THE CREATIVE ART OF

Gift Wrapping

THE CREATIVE ART OF

Gift Wrapping

Rosalind Burdett

Longmeadow Press

The Creative Art of Gift Wrapping

This edition is published by
Longmeadow Press
201 High Ridge Road
Stamford, CT 06904

ISBN 0-681-41005-1

© Salamander Books Ltd. 1987

CREDITS

Editor-in-chief: Jilly Glassborow

Editor: Coral Walker

Designer: Kathy Gummer

Photographer: Steve Tanner

Line artwork: New Leaf Designs

Typeset by: The Old Mill, London

Color separation by: Fotographics Ltd, London – Hong Kong

Printed in Belgium by: Proost International Book Production

0 9 8 7 6 5 4 3 2 1

CONTENTS

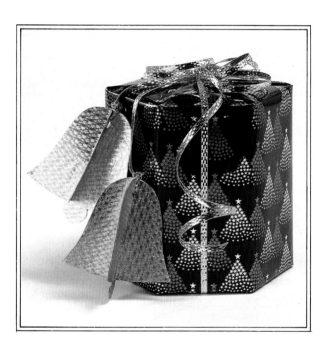

INTRODUCTION

Giving presents is always enjoyable, and the more beautifully wrapped the gift, the greater the pleasure — both to give and to receive. Unfortunately, sometimes wrapping a gift can seem almost as costly as the present itself. This colourful book helps solve the problem with over a hundred bright and clever ideas for wrapping gifts inexpensively and with creative flair, to achieve original and attractive results.

The book begins by showing the basic skills of wrapping different shapes of parcel neatly and stylishly, then progresses through creating and designing personal gift wrap — or adapting ordinary materials such as newspaper — through making (and baking!) tailor-made gift tags, bows, frills and other decorations, to wrapping presents for very special events such as Christmas, birthdays and weddings. There are even novel ways to camouflage obvious gifts such as bottles and records in the guise of trees or kites. Templates appear on pages 124-127 to use for making gift boxes. Each idea is accompanied by illustrated step-by-step instructions to help the reader achieve a stunning effect.

The huge selection of gift wraps on the market should give you plenty of scope for covering your presents. But you don't have to use a ready-made gift wrap — for real individuality and style, you can make your own. The following pages will give you plenty of ideas. For example, what about stencilling your own design, creating a collage, or printing a pattern with a humble potato?

And once you have your wrapping paper, there are lots of tips on how to use it properly, such as how to wrap a cylindrical gift neatly; or what to do with a spherical shape. For more, just read on.

There's no excuse for an unimaginatively wrapped present with such a spectacular range of gift wrap available. Choose from plain, matt, shiny, pastel or bold colours, glossy or glittery designs, to make the most of your gift.

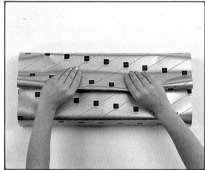

Wrapping square or rectangular presents isn't difficult — but perhaps your technique needs brushing up. Wrap the gift wrap tightly around the box. You can simply stick down the free edge with tape or, for a smarter effect, fold over the top edge of the paper and stick double-sided tape underneath it, leaving a neat fold visible at the join.

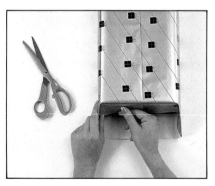

If your paper has a linear design, try to align the design so that the join is not too obvious. Fold the joined section of paper down over the end of the box to make a flap; crease the fold neatly. Trim off any excess paper so there is no unnecessary bulk.

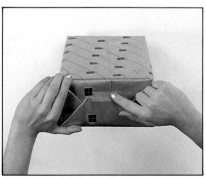

Crease the side flaps firmly, and fold them over the ends of the gift. Smoothing your hand along the side of the box and round on to the end ensures that each flap fits tightly. Fold up the remaining triangular flap, pulling it firmly along the edge of the box, and stick down; use invisible tape (its matt surface is scarcely discernible) or double-sided for the best results.

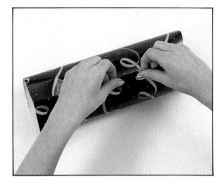

When wrapping a cylinder, avoid using very thick or textured paper as it will be difficult to fold neatly. Cut the paper longer than the cylinder, allowing for extra paper at each end to cover half the cylinder's diameter, and just wider than the gift's circumference. Roll the paper around the parcel and secure with a little tape.

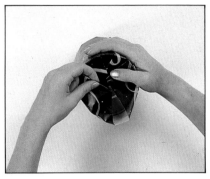

Begin folding the ends of the paper in a series of small triangles as shown here. Continue around the whole circumference, making sure that the 'triangles' are neatly folded into the centre.

Use a single piece of tape at the centre to fix all the folds in place. If the finished folds are not even, you could cheat a little by sticking a circle of matching gift wrap over each end of the cylinder.

The usual method of wrapping a sphere is to gather the paper around the gift and bunch it all together at the top. Here is a more stylish method. Put your circular gift in the centre of a square of paper, checking that the two sides of paper just meet at the top when wrapped around the gift. Cut off the corners of the square to form a circle of paper.

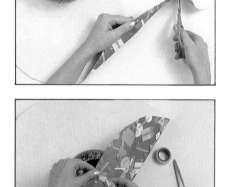

Bring one section of the paper to the top of the gift and begin to pleat it to fit the object as shown. The paper pleats at the top of the gift will end up at more or less the same point; hold them in place every three or four pleats with a tiny piece of sticky tape.

Continue pleating neatly and tightly all the way round the circle. It isn't as complicated or as time-consuming as it sounds once you've got the knack! When you have finished, the pile of pleats on top of the gift should look small and neat. Then you can either cover them with a small circle of paper stuck in place or, more attractively, add a bunch of colourful ribbons.

W rapping awkwardly-shaped presents is just that — awkward. The gift wrap always looks creased and untidy around the angles of the gift. The solution is not to use paper — instead, use brightly-coloured cellophane which doesn't crumple. Cut a square of cellophane a great deal larger than your gift.

Gather the cellophane up and tie it into a bunch above the present. Fan out the excess and add some curled ribbon as a finishing touch. Alternatively, if your gift is cylindrical, roll it in cellophane somewhat longer than the parcel and gather the ends with ribbon.

Stylish, expensive-looking wrapping paper can be achieved very quickly with this method of spray stencilling. Choose some plain coloured paper for a base, and make your stencils from plain cardboard or paper. Cut the stencils into squares of two different sizes; alternatively you could use any kind of basic shape — stars, circles or whatever.

Lay some of the shapes in a random pattern across the plain paper, holding them in place with a spot of Plasticine or modelling clay. Cover the whole paper with paint spray. Use car paint or craft spray paint, but do carry it out in a well-ventilated room.

Once the paint is dry take off the sprayed squares and put a new random pattern of fresh squares across the paper. Overlap some of the original squares with the new ones to create interesting effects, then spray the entire sheet with a second colour of paint. Remove the squares and leave the wrapping paper to dry before using it.

Stencilling is great fun to do — and so easy. Design a simple motif then make a trace of it. With a soft pencil, scribble over the back of the trace and put the tracing paper face up on stencil cardboard. Draw round the design again, pressing hard so that the lines are transferred on to the cardboard beneath. Repeat the motif several times and cut out the shapes with a craft knife.

Position the cut-out stencil on plain paper, and either hold it or use masking tape to keep it in place. Mix up some poster paint, keeping the consistency quite thick. Apply the paint through the stencil, using a stiff brush. When you have finished a row of motifs, lift the stencil carefully and blot it on newspaper so that it is ready to use again. Leave the design to dry.

Keep repeating the process until you have covered enough paper to wrap your gift. To help you keep the spacing even between each run of motifs, add some 'markers' to the stencil. Cut half a motif at the end of the run and another one above the run to mark the position of the next row. Paint the markers along with the other motifs, then use this image for re-positioning the next row.

All kinds of effects can be achieved with a sponge and some paint. You'll need a piece of natural sponge as man-made sponge doesn't produce the right effect. Choose some plain paper and mix up some poster paint to a fairly runny consistency. Test the paint on a spare piece of paper until you're happy with the colour.

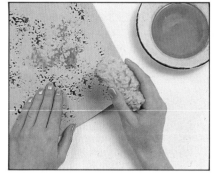

Dab the sponge into the paint and pat it evenly over the paper. The sponge should hold sufficient paint for about four 'dabs' before you need to dip it into the paint again. You'll need to mix up a lot of paint as the sponge absorbs a considerable amount.

Rinse the sponge out well and squeeze dry. When the paper has dried, repeat the process with another colour — you can use as many colours as you wish. Match the ribbon to one of the colours; see page 49 for instructions on how to create the ribbon trim shown here.

SPATTER PATTERNS

This method makes striking wrapping paper — with apologies to artist Jackson Pollock! Creating the pattern is great fun, but rather messy; cover your work area well with an old cloth or waste paper before you start. Begin by mixing up two or more colours in fairly runny poster paint.

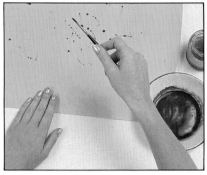

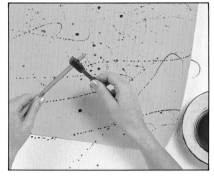

Load a paintbrush with colour, and, with a flicking movement, shake it across the sheet of paper. Repeat several times at various angles to cover the paper. Wait for the paint to dry.

Dip an old toothbrush in another colour paint, avoiding getting the brush too full of liquid. Rub the toothbrush across the blade of a knife to cause the paint to spatter over the paper. Repeat until the spattering is as dense as you like.

Take a tip for decorating your gift from the Victorians, who made glorious scrapbooks and pictures using the art of collage. Collage looks best on plain paper; humble brown paper works admirably. Collect some flower catalogues and you're ready to begin.

From the illustrations of flowers, cut out as many shapes, sizes and colours as you like. Cut fairly accurately around the outline of each flower — it's fiddly, but worth it.

Lay the cut-out flowers on the wrapped parcel. Arrange the pictures in an attractive pattern, then stick them in place with glue. Finally, cut out individual flower petals to form the recipient's name. You can vary this idea by making a collage of a favourite cartoon character for a child or a current pop idol for a teenager.

The ultimate in personalized gift wrapping — write the recipient's name all over it! Choose a plain wrapping paper, and three contrasting felt-tipped pens. Hold the pens together in a row and secure them with sticky tape. Before applying the tape, you must ensure the pens are level so that each pen writes with ease.

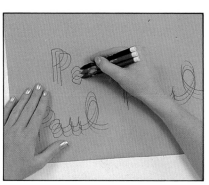

Write the recipient's name randomly across the page in a rounded, flamboyant style. You could vary the effect by grouping the pens in a cluster, rather than a row, or using four or even five pens. Another variation would be to write the name smaller in ordered columns, to give a striped effect.

When you've finished covering the paper with the name, continue the three-tone theme of the gift by tying it up with three ribbons which match the colours of the pens. No one could mistake who this present is for!

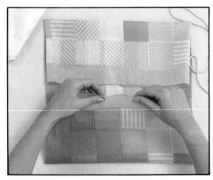

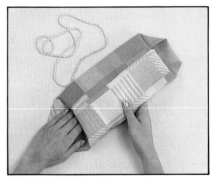

Why not wrap one gift in another? An attractive scarf makes an ideal covering. Fold the edges of the scarf over to make a conveniently-sized square and wrap the scarf around the other gift.

Tuck the top layer of each end of the scarf under the other present as shown, then fold up the end flaps. Use a ribbon or string of beads to hold the flaps in place. Alternatively, a couple of pretty handkerchiefs make a good wrapping for a small gift such as soap. Gather the hankies around the gift and secure in a bunch with a length of lace.

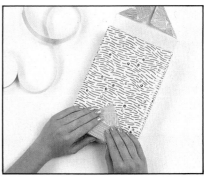

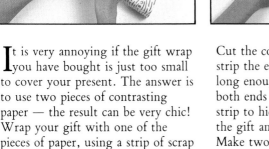

It is very annoying if the gift wrap you have bought is just too small to cover your present. The answer is to use two pieces of contrasting paper — the result can be very chic! Wrap your gift with one of the pieces of paper, using a strip of scrap paper to protect the gift from the tape. Fold in the ends neatly.

Cut the contrasting gift wrap into a strip the exact width of your parcel, long enough to cover the back and both ends plus two flaps. Use this strip to hide the uncovered back of the gift and fold it over the two ends. Make two flaps on the front of the parcel as shown and secure with double-sided tape. Alternatively, wrap each end of the parcel in different paper, hiding the join with a ribbon.

Glittering wrapping paper is always glamorous, and with glitter available in such a variety of colours your creativity need know no bounds! Spread out a sheet of plain coloured paper and, using a bottle of glue with a fine nozzle, draw a series of simple patterns across it.

Sprinkle a line of glitter across the paper. Tip up the sheet and gently shake all the glitter from one side of the paper to the other, across the glued designs, making sure that all the patterns have been well covered. Tip the excess glitter off the page on to a sheet of newspaper; the glitter can then be used again.

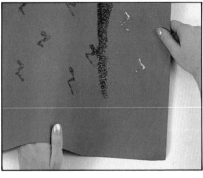

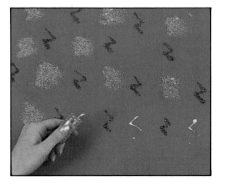

Now use the glue to make more designs and coat these in glitter of a different colour. Localize the sprinkling of the glitter over the new patterns to be covered and leave to dry. Tip off the excess glitter and return it to its container.

Employ a humble potato to create simple yet beautiful designs. Begin by cutting a large potato in half and draw a simple design on it. Use a sharp knife or craft knife to sculp the potato, leaving the design raised from the surface.

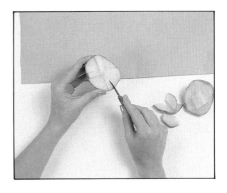

To ensure a regular print, draw a grid lightly in pencil on a sheet of plain paper. Then mix up fairly thick poster paint and apply it to the potato-cut with a paintbrush. Print the design in the middle of each square of the grid. You should be able to do two or three prints before the colour fades and needs replenishing.

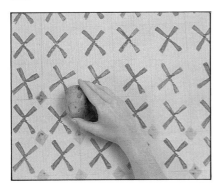

Cover the whole sheet with one design. Cut another design on another potato half; repeat the whole process, this time printing on the cross of the grid. When the paint is thoroughly dry, rub out the grid lines still visible and wrap up your present.

Wallpaper borders can look very effective on any square- or rectangular-shaped gift. Cut a strip of border the length of one side of your wrapped gift; glue it in place along the edge.

Cut another border strip for an adjacent edge. Apply glue, and position the strip so that the end of it overlaps the first strip. Now mitre the overlapped corners by trimming the top strip at an angle. Do this by ruling a line between the corner of the gift and the point at which the strips overlap, as shown here.

Cut off the excess triangle of wallpaper border with a craft knife. Don't press too hard or you could damage the gift underneath. Cut two matching border strips for the other edges of the gift and repeat the mitring process with the remaining three corners.

W allpaper is often useful as a gift covering — particularly if your present is very large. Here we have used thick wallpaper with an embossed pattern and given it a touch of style and individuality. Wrap your gift, and choose some wax crayons in contrasting shades. Rub a colour over the raised surface of the wallpaper to highlight one of the motifs in the design.

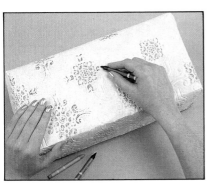

Choose another colour, and use it to pick out another section in the pattern. (Instead of wax crayons, you could use coloured pencils or chalk; the latter would need to be rubbed with a tissue afterwards to remove loose dust. The medium you choose must slide over the embossing without colouring in the whole design — paint is therefore not suitable.)

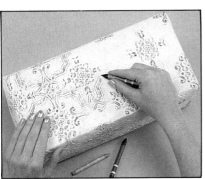

Repeat the process using a third colour and continue with as many shades as you like. A tip while wrapping your gift — you'll probably find that ordinary tape will not stick to the surface of wallpaper; double-sided tape used between two folds will be more effective.

Brightly-coloured adhesive tape can give any plain wrapping paper a touch of style. A geometric design is easiest to create with tape, and the most effective; curves are rather difficult! Work out your design first and measure it out accurately on the parcel in pencil.

Stick the tapes in place along the pencil marks. Take care that the tapes don't stretch at all during application or they will cause the paper to pucker slightly. Sticky tapes are available in an enormous variety of colours, textures and patterns; choose a strong contrast with your paper.

DELICATE DOILIES

The delicate silhouette of a doily against a contrasting background colour looks attractive on a gift. Wrap your present up in plain paper and glue the doilies wherever you like. To decorate the corners of a large gift, fold a doily in half, then in half again.

Unfold the doily carefully and spread it out. Cut off one of the quarters of the doily; the folds along which you should cut will be clearly visible.

Paste the doily over one corner of the gift as shown. Repeat with alternate corners, unless your gift has enough space to take a doily over each corner without overlap. The doilies don't have to be white: silver or gold is also effective. Nor do they have to be circular — square ones would be smart on a square-sided present.

If the present you've bought is an awkward shape, why waste time and energy trying to wrap it up neatly? Make a box — or a bag — and just pop your gift inside. No more fuss or effort! And the person who receives your gift gets a bonus, since he or she can use the box or bag again afterwards.

On the following pages, there are instructions for making twelve different cardboard boxes, and two kinds of fabric bags. The patterns for the boxes can be found on pages 124-127, and by scaling them up or down you can make a box of any size you like.

Why not try your hand at making a container from this smart selection of gift boxes and bags. They are totally professional in finish, yet remarkably straightforward to make.

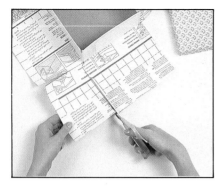

When re-covered in plastic, a shoe box makes a great container for a present. Put the box in the centre of a piece of self-adhesive plastic and draw around it. Then draw around the shape of the sides and ends of the box so you end up with a diagram of the 'exploded' box. Allow extra plastic all round for overlaps. Cut out the pattern you have just created.

Peel the backing off the plastic and position the box carefully in the middle of the covering. Smooth the rest of the plastic up over the box, starting with the ends. Wrap the small overlap around the corners as shown.

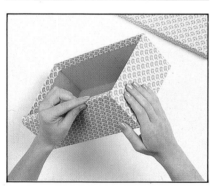

Smooth the plastic up over the sides, trimming off the edges to make the pieces the exact size of the sides. Fold over the overlaps around the rim. Cover the lid in the same way. For complete co-ordination, you could cover the inside of the box to match. Alternatively, you could line the box with co-ordinating tissue paper or net.

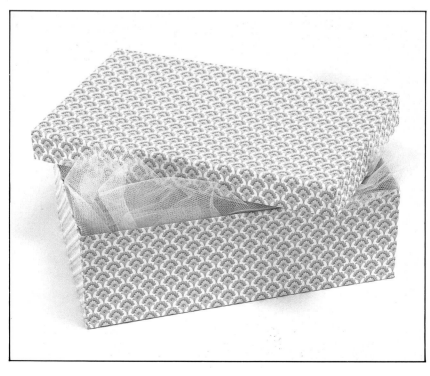

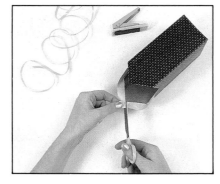

A handy gift container, ideal for home-made sweets, can be made from a well-washed juice carton. Draw V-shapes in each side of the carton. These should be inverted on two opposite sides, and pointing towards the top of the carton on the other two sides. Cut cleanly along the drawn lines with a craft knife as shown.

Cover the carton with gift wrap; adhesive in spray form achieves the best results. Make sure the join lies neatly down one corner of the box. Trim the overlap at the top of the carton so that it is even and fold the paper over the edges, taking care that the corners are neat. Punch a hole at the apex of both the pointed sides and thread ribbon through.

This cube-shaped box is ideal for containing any kind of gift and it can be made to any size. Measure out the shape of the box on to thin cardboard, following the template on page 124. It's very important that all the squares are exactly the same size and that all the angles are right angles. Cut out the shape, and score along the fold lines — the back of a craft knife is useful for doing this.

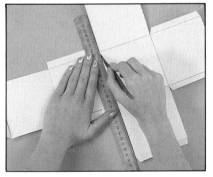

Bend the card carefully along the score lines, making a neat crease along each fold. Crease the flaps on the lid and base and fold the four sides into the shape of the box.

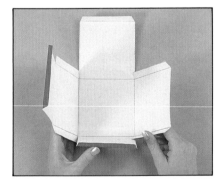

Stick the side flap to its opposite side as shown. You can glue this, or alternatively, use double-sided tape. Fold in the base flap — it should fit precisely and thus give the box rigidity. Finally close the lid flap.

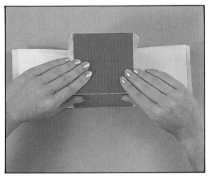

Making a box from scratch can be a little complicated, so why not start with an empty cereal packet? Take your cereal packet and carefully open it out flat. Separating the joins needs care — if necessary slide a knife between the seams to part the glue, rather than tear the packet.

Draw the box you want, using the template on page 124 as a reference. Make sure the lid measures the same as the width of the side panels. Cut out the new shape with a pair of scissors, and cover it with your chosen gift wrap. Spray adhesive is best, since this gives a very smooth finish, however glue in a stick form will do. When the glue has dried, cut neatly around the cardboard shape.

Score along the new fold lines of the box using the back of a craft knife or the blunt edge of a pair of scissors. Fold the box into shape. Stick the side flap in place as shown; you can use double-sided tape or glue. Fix the two flaps on the bottom (either glue or tape them). Put in some shredded tissue as padding, slot in your gift and tuck the lid neatly into place.

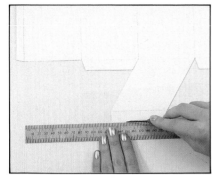

A variation on the cube gives this box an unusual diamond shape. Draw the template on page 125 on to thin coloured cardboard. Check that all the sides are the same size, and that their angles measure 90°; the angles of the lid and base should measure about 60° and 120°. Cut out the shape with a craft knife.

Score along the fold lines on the sides and flaps of the box with the back of a craft knife or the blunt edge of a pair of scissors. Fold the scored edges over, making sure that they are well creased for a crisp shape.

Fit the box together, sticking down the side flap with glue or double-sided tape. Fold in the base and the lid; it is the shape of these which converts the box from being an ordinary cube into the more exotic diamond shape.

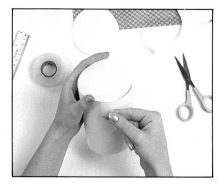

A cylindrical box looks much more difficult to make than it is. Wrap a piece of thin cardboard around the gift to determine the measurement of the box. Cut out the cardboard, roll it up and stick down the edge with a length of tape. Draw and cut out a circular base, and a slightly larger circle for the lid. Attach the base with small bits of tape.

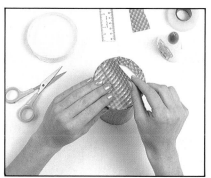

Cut a strip of cardboard slightly longer than the circumference of the cylinder. To make the lid, stick the edge of the strip to the edge of the circle with tape. Next, spread glue on some gift wrap and roll the cylinder in it. Cut the paper to fit, allowing an overlap each end. Tuck the overlap into the open end; secure. Fold the base overlap in a series of small triangles and stick to the base.

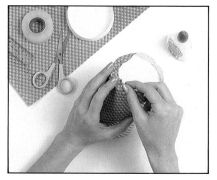

Draw a circle of gift wrap slightly smaller than the base. Cut it out and glue in position, hiding all the folds and bits of tape. Cover the lid in the same way. If you like, you can punch two holes in each side of the container and thread through short lengths of decorative braid.

This attractive and unusual bag will add prestige to any present. Draw the template featured on page 125 on to a sheet of thin cardboard with the aid of a compass and a protractor; use a pencil as some of the design will need to be erased later. Cut out the circle and score along the lines of the 'star' and the central octagon with a sharp edge — the back of a craft knife will do.

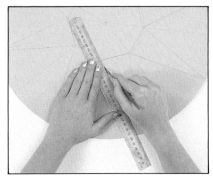

Take care not to overscore along the intersections of the lines, as the cardboard could eventually tear. Rub out any line not scored. Bend along the edges of the octagon, being careful not to crease the sides. Then fold along the arms of the 'star', to form a series of triangles (these will come together to form the container for your gift).

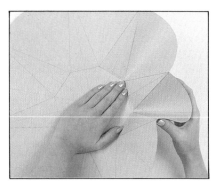

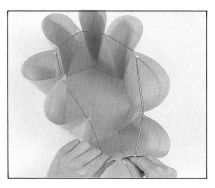

Folding the box needs patience, but it's not as complicated as it looks! When the folding is complete, punch holes either side of the top of each triangle (see the template) and thread the ribbon through the holes as shown. Arrange the curved edges so that they radiate out from the centre. You can make the bag any size you want; as a guide, though, ours had a diameter of 40cm (16in).

Smart handles give this box style; they are also the mechanism for closing it. Use coloured cardboard for the box; if you try to cover the box pattern with gift wrap it will lift off. Copy the template on page 126, scaling it up or down if you wish. Use a compass to draw the handles. Cut out the shape with a craft knife, taking great care with the handles and their slots.

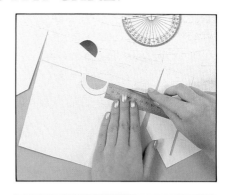

Score along all the fold lines using the back of a craft knife; crease them well. Fold the carton into shape, and stick down the side flap with double-sided tape or glue. Fold the base down, pushing the flap inside the box to secure it.

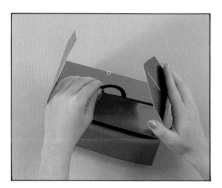

Close the first two flaps of the lid, folding the handles up to fit. Pinch the handles together and fold the two top flaps of the lid over them, fitting the handles through the slots.

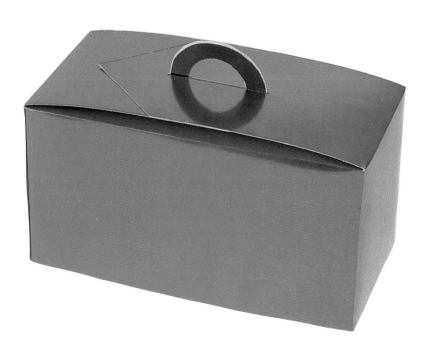

A plant is a notoriously difficult item to wrap; here's a smart solution. Measure an equilateral triangle on some coloured cardboard. The length of each side should be twice the height of the plant; use a protractor to ensure all the angles measure 60°.

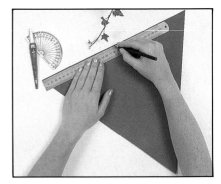

Divide each of the three sides of the triangle in half. Join all the half marks together to form an inner equilateral triangle; this will form the base. Bend the card along a ruler at each inner line as shown and bring up the sides to form a three-dimensional triangle. Punch a hole in each apex and thread ribbon through to close the parcel; double length ribbon gives a pretty finishing touch.

These rigid little boxes are ideal for presenting jewellery but you can make them to fit anything you like. Choose thin cardboard, either in the colour you want the finished box to be, or white so that you can cover it later with gift wrap. Measure out the template on page 126. The size of the triangular sides doesn't matter, as long as they are all the same, and the base is a true square.

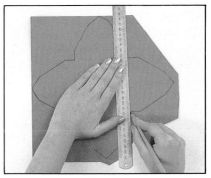

Cut out along the exterior lines with a craft knife. If you're covering the cardboard shape with gift wrap, do it at this stage, cutting the paper to fit. Score along all the fold lines carefully, using the back of the craft knife, then bend the box along the score marks, creasing firmly.

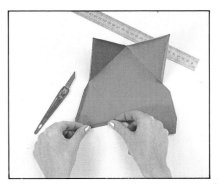

Punch holes in each apex and fold the box into its pyramidal shape. Thread the ribbon in and out of the four holes and, making sure all the side-folds are tucked inside the box, tie the loose ends together with a bow.

T his method is best suited to a small box as the end result is not particularly strong. From thin cardboard, cut out a cross-shaped piece as shown, made up of four sides and a base, all the same size and all absolutely square. The lid will also be a square measuring 5mm (¼in) larger than the base, with sides about 2cm (¾in) deep.

Paste both shapes on to gift wrap and when dry cut off the gift wrap around the box and lid, leaving a small turning or flap around each edge. Fold in the flap on the left of each side of the box and glue it down as shown. Score along the edges of what will be the base, to form fold lines for the sides of the box.

Bend the sides upwards. Put glue on the patterned side of the flaps of gift wrap left unfolded on each side; stick these flaps inside the box to the adjacent sides as illustrated. Crease down the sides firmly and leave to dry. Finally, fold in and glue the top lip. Treat the lid in exactly the same way.

These sachets are ideal for ties, soaps, scarves, jewellery, hankies, socks and so forth. On to thin cardboard, trace the template on page 127. It's probably more interesting to cover the shape with gift wrap as shown here, but you can use plain cardboard if you wish. If using gift wrap, cut out the shape and paste it on to your chosen wrapping paper.

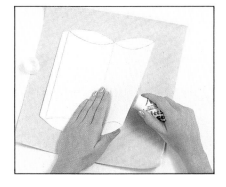

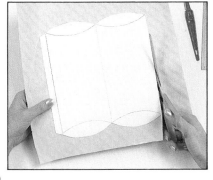

Cut out the covered shape. Then score well along the curved lines of the ellipses which will form the overlapping ends of the packet. Use the back of a craft knife or the blunt side of a pair of scissors to make the score marks.

Stick the side flaps together with either double-sided tape or glue. Fold in the ends; if you've scored the lines sufficiently they should pop in easily with just a little guidance. They can be re-opened with no difficulty, but make sure the covering gift wrap doesn't begin to lift off the cardboard.

This small narrow box would be ideal for giving someone a watch or a piece of jewellery — unless, of course, you make it bigger! Trace off the template on page 127 on to thin cardboard. Cut it out, and either cover it in gift wrap or, if you like the colour of the cardboard, just leave it plain.

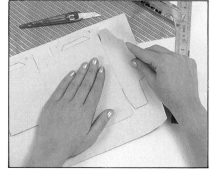

Cut around the template with small sharp scissors to trim away the excess gift wrap; take extra care with the slots and handles. Then score along all the fold lines, using the back of the craft knife or the blunt edge of the scissors.

Crease all the folds properly. Fold the box into shape and stick the side flap to the inside of the opposite side. Close the top section, being sure to fold the lid sections upright as shown, halfway across at the point where the two handles meet. Fold over the end flaps and slot them in position to close the box. Finally close the base.

Gift bags are very useful as containers for awkwardly-shaped presents and they can be made to any size. Find something with the required dimensions of the finished bag to serve as a mould — a pile of books should suffice. Choose a good quality, strong gift wrap for making the bag. Cut a strip of gift wrap long enough to wrap round the 'mould' and fold over the top edge.

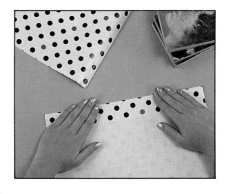

Wrap the paper round the mould; glue or use double-sided tape to join the seam at the back. Fold over the end flaps in the usual way of wrapping any parcel to make the base of the bag; be sure to attach sufficient tape to make the base strong.

Slip the mould out. Fold in the sides of the bag, creasing them in half at the top; fold the base up over the back of the bag. Punch two holes, spaced apart, at the top of the front and back of the bag as shown. Thread through a length of cord to form a handle; knot each end inside the bag. Repeat on the other side. Alternatively, you could thread the bag with ribbon.

A few pretty soaps are a doubly welcome gift when wrapped in one of these pretty fabric draw-string bags. Cut a strip of cotton fabric about 5cm (2in) wider than you want the finished bag to be, and about 10cm (4in) longer. Turn in about 5cm (2in) at the top of each edge and run a double line of stitching along it to form a channel for the draw-strings.

Pin the side seams with the right sides of the fabric together, making sure the tops of both sides match. Sew the seams, leaving a gap at each end of the draw-string channel. If you don't have a sewing machine, the sewing can be done easily by hand.

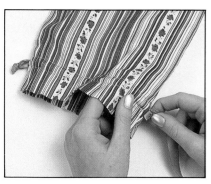

Turn the bag right side out and press it. Get some ribbon four times longer than the width of the bag and cut it in half. Attach a safety pin to the end of one half; thread it and the ribbon through the channels around the top of the bag so that both ends come out of one side. Knot the ends. Thread the other ribbon through both channels too, so the ends come from the other side; knot these too.

A flat gift can be slipped into this pretty and useful fabric envelope. Make a paper pattern measuring about 5cm (2in) wider than your gift and two and a half times its depth, cutting a shallow V-shape at one end for the flap. Fold your fabric in half and position the paper pattern with the straight edge opposite the pointed end on the fold. Pin it on and cut the fabric out.

With right sides of the fabric together, pin and sew around the edges, leaving a small opening of about 7.5cm (3in); this is to enable the bag to be turned inside out. Turn the bag and press it. Then sew up the gap which was left. You can of course sew all this by hand if you prefer.

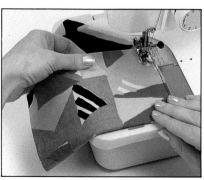

Fold the strip into an envelope shape, with the pointed flap at the top. Pin up the edges carefully and sew them in position with a double row of stitching as shown. Sew a length of ribbon on to the back of the bag with a couple of smaller stitches, pop in the present and tie the ribbon in a bow at the front.

The decorative details on a gift can make all the difference to the finished article. The gift wrap might be bright and jolly, but if the present has no decoration it can look very dull. Even a pretty bow can provide the finishing touch, turning a plain parcel into a chic gift.

Buying ribbon pom-poms can make gift wrapping very expensive. Instead, try making your own decorations. In this section you'll find instructions for ten different kinds of ribbon decoration. And why stop at ribbons? What about tassels, foil stars, paper ruffles, and flowers of all kinds? Here are more than 30 imaginative ideas.

Reels of gift ribbon can be turned into a
vast array of different decorations; from
stunning rosettes that you couldn't
distinguish from shop-bought versions to
individual and original pom-poms. Braid,
cord, tissues and even candy can be used
to decorate your gifts and make parcels
that extra bit special.

Here is an easy way to achieve a very pretty effect. Choose three colours of narrow ribbon which co-ordinate with your gift wrap. Using one ribbon, tie it around your parcel in the usual way, crossing it underneath the parcel and knotting it tightly on top; leave long ends. Tie a length of different coloured ribbon to the centre point, then do the same with a third colour.

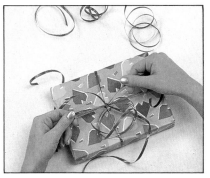

Continue tying on lengths of ribbon so that you end up with two lengths, (that is, four ends) of each colour. Tie the central knots tightly to keep them as small as possible. Pull a ribbon length gently along the open blade of a pair of scissors; this will cause it to curl into ringlets. Repeat with each length until they are as curly as you want.

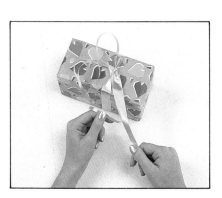

An alternative is to use wide gift ribbon. Tie it round the parcel once, making sure that the knot is as neat as possible and leaving long ends. Cut two small nicks in the ribbon, dividing it evenly into three; pull it to split the ribbon up to the knot. Run each of these lengths along the blade of a pair of scissors until they form ringlets.

A pom-pom bow adds a cheerful touch to a present of any shape or size. Use the kind of ribbon which will stick to itself when moistened. Cut seven strips; four measuring about 30cm (12in), the other three about 23cm (9in). You'll also need a small piece of ribbon about 5cm (2in), for the central loop.

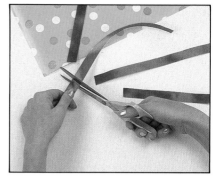

Overlap the ends of each of the long strips and moisten them; stick them together to form a loop. Moisten the centre of each loop and stick it together as shown. Cross two of the looped strips, joining them at the central point. Repeat with the other two loops. Join both crosses together so the loops are evenly spaced apart.

Loop the three shorter lengths, and cross them over each other, fixing them together at the centre. Stick the resulting star in the middle of the large rosette. Fill in the centre with the tiny loop. Obviously, the length and width of ribbon can be varied, according to the size you want the finished pom-pom to be.

The scrolled shapes of this
decoration are reminiscent of the
curlicues embellishing Queen
Elizabeth I's signature. Wrap up
your present, and choose some gift
wrapping ribbon to match or
contrast with the colours of the gift
wrap. Hold the end of the ribbon in
one hand, and form a loop as shown,
leaving a small tail.

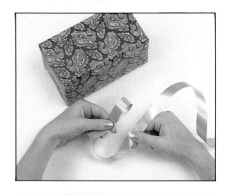

Make a corresponding loop below,
forming a figure-of-eight shape. This
will be the size of the finished
product; adjust the proportion of the
loops at this stage if you want a
bigger or smaller bow. Continue
folding loops of the same size until
you have as many as you want —
seven at each end is usually enough.

Check that all the loops are the same
size, and pinch them all together by
wrapping a piece of sticky tape
around the middle. You can then
hide this by wrapping a small piece
of matching ribbon over it. Attach it
to the present with double-sided
tape.

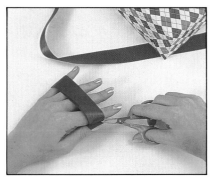

T̲his bow, with its floppy loops,
gives a soft, casual effect. You'll
need about 2m (6ft) of acetate or
craft ribbon, 2.5cm (1in) wide. Cut
off about 30cm (12in) ribbon; wind
the rest round your fingers. Holding
the ribbon firmly, make a notch in
both edges with a pair of scissors as
shown, cutting through all the layers
of ribbon.

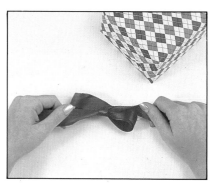

Take the ribbon off your hand and
notch the edges of the opposite side
of the loops. Flatten the loops so that
the notches match in the centre and
loops are formed either side. Take
the 30cm (12in) length of ribbon and
tie it tightly around the notches as
shown.

Starting with the innermost loop on
one side of the folded bow, gently
pull each loop away from the other
loops and into the centre of the bow.
You'll end up with each loop being
visible, thus forming the shape of the
finished rosette.

This trimming can be made to match or contrast with the wrapping. You will need the type of ribbon which sticks to itself when dampened; choose whatever colours you like. The smallest strip of ribbon measures about 20cm (8in); cut it out and twist it into the shape of a figure '8'.

Twist the ribbon shape to form a point at each end as shown, then secure it in position by dampening the tape. Cut the next strip, about 7.5cm (3in) bigger; repeat the process. Put the smaller shape on top and in the centre of the new shape; fix it in place.

Make four other figures-of-eight, cutting each one about 7.5cm (3in) longer than the last. Pile them all up and fix them together in the centre. Put the decoration on your gift and attach it by wrapping ribbon round it and the parcel. Finally, arrange it so that each loop is raised above the others and not overlapping as they're inclined to do!

Silky tassels give a luxurious look to a gift, especially if they are made of sparkling Lurex yarn. Cut a piece of thin cardboard the length you'd like the tassels to be. Wind yarn around the cardboard until it's the density you had in mind for the finished tassel.

Thread a length of yarn through all the strands. Tie it firmly at the top of the cardboard as shown, leaving the ends long. Cut through the strands of yarn at the opposite end of the cardboard.

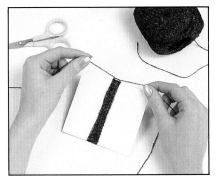

Tie some yarn around the tassel, about 1cm (½in) from the top; trim the ends to the length of the tassel fringe. Make another tassel. Twist together four long lengths of yarn and tie them round the parcel in the usual way; tie the tassels at each end. Ordinary yarn or thick rug yarn would look just as effective.

Y ou couldn't distinguish this pointed pom-pom from a shop-bought version — yet it's a fraction of the price! Use ribbon which sticks to itself when moistened. Make a small loop by wrapping the ribbon round your thumb; moisten the ribbon and fix it in place. Now twist the ribbon back on itself to form a pointed loop, as shown; stick it in position.

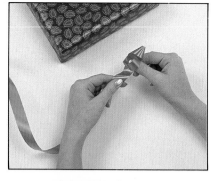

Go on looping the ribbon in twists, spacing them evenly as you go. It is fairly fiddly but keep trying — you'll soon master the technique. You'll probably need to wait a minute between each fixing for the ribbon's glue to dry before turning the next loop.

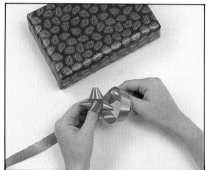

Continue winding outwards in a circle until the bow is as big as you want; cut off the ribbon, leaving a small tail just visible. Attach the pom-pom to the present with double-sided tape.

It's hard to believe that these pretty flowers and the butterfly are made from tights (pantyhose) and fuse wire. Cut up a pair of discarded tights or stockings. Cut some 15 amp fuse wire into lengths, some shorter than others, suitable for making petals. Make a circular shape out of each length and twist the ends together.

Put a piece of stocking material over a wire circle and pull it tight, making sure that the whole circle is covered. Fix it in position by firmly winding matching cotton around the twisted stem of the wire. Cut off the excess fabric.

Take seven petals, smaller ones in the centre, and bind them all tightly with thread. Bend the petals around until you're happy with the look of the flower. Tie up your parcel with ribbon and attach the flower with double-sided tape. The butterfly is made in just the same way: two pairs of 'petals' are bound together with thread, then bent into the shape of wings.

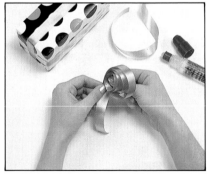

How to give a tall thin present
even more presence! Take a
spool of gift ribbon — the sort that
sticks to itself when moistened. Roll
a length round your thumb to form
a small circle; moisten and stick in
position.

Make another ring, larger than the
first; stick that down too. Make
another circle, and another, ensuring
that their increase in size is in the
same proportion each time. Four
circles is about the maximum the
ribbon can take before flopping
slightly and thus losing the crispness
of the decoration.

SEQUIN SHEEN

The metallic sheen of sequins, and the strip of metallic plastic from which they are pressed, looks rather chic. Sequin waste — that is, the strip of metallic plastic — can be bought by the metre or yard from good craft shops. This idea looks best on rectangular flat parcels. Wrap a piece of sequin waste around the length of the present; fix it with tape.

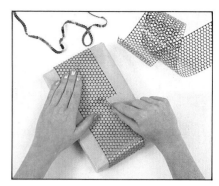

Take another strip of sequin waste and join the two ends to make a large loop. Use sticky tape to fix them, making sure the holes overlap so that the join is almost invisible.

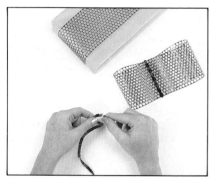

Put a strip of threaded sequin trim of the same colour across the middle of the loop. Remove a few loose sequins so that you can tie the trim in position. Repeat with another length of trim; space the two evenly apart in the centre of the loop to form a bow. Attach the bow to the parcel with double-sided tape. Sequin trim as a gift tie in its own right gives a glamorous finish to any gift.

This decoration looks best on a rectangular gift. Take 66cm (26in) of woven ribbon; lay it flat. Measure 13cm (5in) from one end of the ribbon and mark both edges. Then mark along the ribbon's length a further 10cm (4in), 7.5cm (3in), 5cm (2in), 7.5cm (3in), 10cm (4in). Using one piece of thread, pick up tiny stitches at each mark along one edge.

Run a similar gathering thread up the other edge of ribbon, making sure that the stitches are exactly level on both sides. Gather up the loops as shown; it's easiest to knot the two threads together at one end of the gathers and ease the loops along.

Pull the thread tight to make properly-formed loops; sew the joins in place and cut off the excess thread. Tie the ribbon around the gift and use double-sided tape to attach the loops in the centre of the long side of the gift. Snip a diagonal cut at the ends of the ribbon tails.

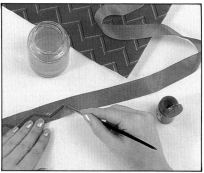

It is quite easy to paint wide ribbon to co-ordinate with your wrapping paper. And the results are stunning! Choose a gift wrap with a simple design. Decide whether you want the ribbon to be a positive version of the paper's design, like the blue example shown here, or a negative one, like the black and white suggestions. Experiment with poster paint on your chosen ribbon.

Keep the design very simple and stylized. When you're happy with your pattern, paint enough ribbon to wrap up the gift, allowing sufficient for a fairly large bow. Leave the ribbon to dry thoroughly before tying it around the parcel. If the paint does crack a little when tying up the ribbon, simply touch it up and leave it to dry again.

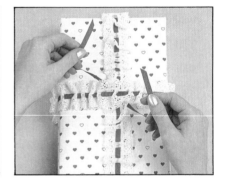

For an elaborate and slightly saucy effect for your present, select some slotted lace and some ribbon to co-ordinate with your gift wrap. Measure the amount of ribbon needed to tie up the parcel; you will need twice as much lace. Thread the ribbon through the slots.

Gather the lace up on the ribbon. Wrap it round the length of the parcel and sew it together at the back. Then wrap the width; sew that too. Finish by tying an extra bow at the intersection of the two laces. Any present looks pretty simply tied with lace, even if the lace can prove a little expensive. Look out for remnants in haberdashery (notions) departments or market stalls.

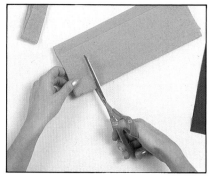

C repe paper is the ideal material to make a stylish ruffle. There's such a range of colours to choose from, too. For each ruffle, cut two strips of crepe paper, one a little wider than the other. They should both be half as long again as the circumference of the parcel.

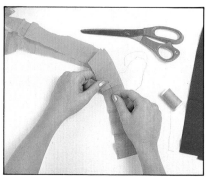

Lay the two strips flat, with the narrower one on top. Sew them both together with matching thread, running a gathering thread down the centre. Gather the strips slightly.

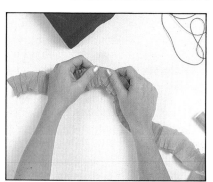

Gently stretch the crepe between both hands along the entire length of the strip; this will create a more ruffled effect. Do each strip separately, then make another ruffle. Wrap the ruffles around the gift, sticking the ends with tape. Tie narrow cord in the middle of the strips to hide the gathering stitches; fluff up the crepe ruffles either side.

Pick out the colours of your gift wrap to make your own pretty plaits. From narrow fabric ribbon — 2mm (¹/₈in) wide — choose either three colours which feature in your wrapping paper or, if your prefer, three lengths of the same shade. Knot them together at one end, leaving small tails.

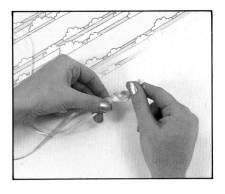

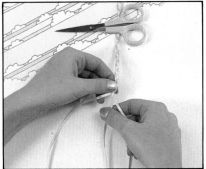

Start plaiting the ribbon. This is easier if you weigh down the knot with something; the scissors will do fine. Keep plaiting as evenly as possible, moving the weight along the growing length of plait as necessary.

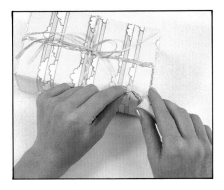

When you've finished, tie the plait round your gift in the usual way. Before knotting it, undo the knot you made when you began plaiting; tie a single tight knot to keep both ends of the plait in place. Loop each tail back on itself, dabbing on a tiny spot of glue and fixing it in the centre beside the knot.

This elegant two-tone cord with its matching rosette is made of twisted ric-rac. Choose two colours of ric-rac braid to co-ordinate with your wrapping paper; buy about 1m (3ft) of both colours. Wrap one piece of braid around the zig-zags of the other, twisting them so that they fit snugly together. Do enough to wrap around your gift and press the braid with a cool iron.

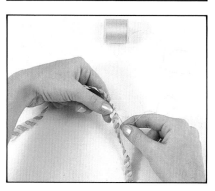

Twist some more braid together to make the rosette — the length you need depends on the size of the rosette. Take a needle and thread through each point of one side of the twisted ric-rac.

Having threaded about 45cm (18in), gently pull the thread, easing it along the ric-rac. This will cause the ric-rac to coil up on itself; arrange it into a flat circle, sewing it together as you go. When you have a large enough rosette, cut the braid and sew the edges neatly under. Tie the long length of braid around the parcel and sew in position; sew on the rosette.

A winning idea for any gift! Cut a length of fairly wide ribbon; you'll need about 30cm (12in) for each rosette. Fold it in half with the right sides of the ribbon together; sew up the two ends to form a seam.

Using tiny stitches, gather up one edge of the ribbon. Pull the gathering thread tight, arranging the rosette into a neat circle as you do so. Finish it off by sewing across the base. Make as many rosettes as you need and attach them to your parcel with double-sided tape.

ROSEBUDS

A small posy of pretty rosebuds is always acceptable — make as many as you like! Cut a small length of ribbon — about 6-9cm (2-3½in), depending on the width of ribbon you've chosen. Fold the ribbon in half, right sides together, and join the two ends with a small seam. Run a gathering thread around one edge.

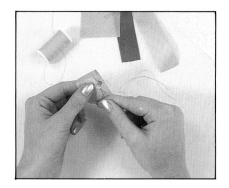

Pull the gathering thread tight to form the rosebud; sew it firmly across the base. Make another two or three buds and sew them all together at the base; you may need to add the occasional supporting stitch at the top edges to hold the buds close together.

The leaves add an attractive contrast. They are made from a strip of green ribbon, two corners of which have been folded over to form a point. Fix with double-sided tape since glue can leave a mark on ribbon. The illustration below shows the rosebuds grouped on a length of ribbon twice the width of the flowers, set off with narrow green ribbon.

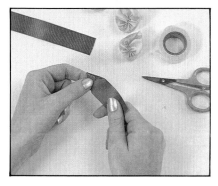

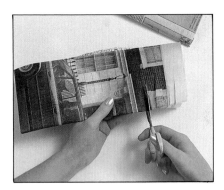

What do you do when you haven't any gift wrap and the shops are shut? You use newspaper! The flower on top gives the parcel a stunning and stylish finish. To create the flower cut several lengths of newspaper, some about 15cm (6in) wide, some a little narrower. Fold one strip in half lengthways, and make a series of cuts along its folded edge as shown here.

When you've cut along the whole length, roll up the resulting looped fringe. Secure it at the base by winding a piece of sticky tape round it. Fluff out the 'petals' of the flower.

Use up all the strips of paper in the same way. Gather the sections together, smaller ones on the outside. Join them all with tape; leave the ends unstuck and use them to attach the flower to the gift. You can even match the paper to the recipient; use a financial newspaper for a businessman, a comic for a child, a glossy magazine for a lady of leisure.

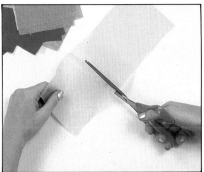

You can make these decorations in a single colour, but they look more effective if you choose several. For each twist, you need three squares of tissue for the outer colour, two for the middle colour and two for the inner (most visible) section. The squares needed for the inner section are smaller than those for the outside; the middle leaves must be of a size in between.

Pick up the squares in order, putting one on top of the other; outer colour first, then the middle, then the inner squares. Position them so that the corners of each square are at a different angle, as shown. Put a couple of stitches through the centre point to secure all the squares together and leave some thread hanging.

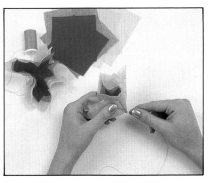

Fold the whole thing in half and half again, twisting the folded point at the base to form the shape of the 'flower'. Pull the thread out at the point, and wind it tightly around the twisted base to secure it; 'fluff' out the finished decoration. Make several 'flowers' and group them together on your present.

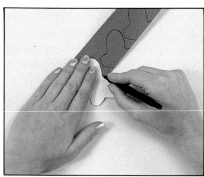

An interesting effect is achieved by attaching three-dimensional decorations all over your parcel. Wrap your gift in plain coloured paper. For the butterflies, take a strip of contrasting plain paper and fold it in half. Draw a butterfly shape on thin cardboard; cut it out and trace round half of it as shown on to the coloured paper. Draw as many as you want to cover the gift.

Cut out the butterfly shapes and fold them on both sides of the half-way fold, to give them bodies. Use glue or thin strips of double-sided tape to attach them in a random pattern to the parcel. Alternatively, tie lots of little bows of the same size using contrasting ribbon; scatter them over your gift using double-sided tape.

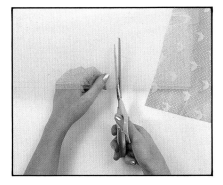

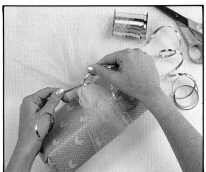

Frothy net is a very attractive decorative feature, and silver glitter adds a sparkle and a touch of glamour. Cut a strip of net long enough to wrap twice around the perimeter of the gift; make its breadth about 15cm (6in) wider than the length of the parcel.

Gather the net in small pleats and wrap it around the middle of the parcel, as shown. Tie the net with narrow gift ribbon and leave the ends of the ribbon trailing. Gently pull apart the net tails. Cut another piece of net the same width as the first piece and twice the height of the existing 'frill'; thread it underneath the frill and secure it with ribbon as before.

Put some silver glitter in a bowl and dab glue along the raw edges of the net. Dip the net in to the glitter (this involves holding the parcel upside down). Shake off the excess glitter and allow the glue to dry. Curl up the trailing lengths of ribbon by pulling them against a scissor blade.

WILD ABOUT WINDMILLS

Windmills are cheerful and fun for people of all ages — not just children! Cut out a square of plain coloured paper which complements your wrapping paper. Measure a square of about 23cm (9in), depending on the size of windmill you want; make sure the corners are right angles. Cut out the square and draw straight lines between the opposite corners.

Cut along these lines, starting from the corners and leaving about 2.5cm (1in) uncut in the centre. Bend up one side of each cut corner to the centre, as shown, anchoring it with double-sided tape.

To attach the windmill to a 'pole', take a coloured plastic drinking straw and insert a two-pronged paper fastener in the end; open the prongs out a little so the fastener stays firm. Pierce the centre of the windmill with another paper fastener; pass its prongs through the one inserted in the straw before opening them out. Attach the straw and windmill to the parcel with double-sided tape.

A smartly-dressed present for a smartly-dressed man — or woman! This is suitable for a tall thin gift. Wrap it up in paper of a colour and design that is plausible for a shirt. Cut out a 'collar' shape as shown from stiff white paper; fix it in position around the top of the parcel with glue or double-sided tape.

Using patterned ribbon for the tie (such as this elegant paisley design), wrap it around the collar and knot it like a tie. Before pulling it tight, put some glue or double-sided tape on the collar where the tie should sit; position the tie correctly and tighten the knot. Finally, fold over the two corners of the collar shape to make an elegantly formal shirt; make sure the collar is even.

A pretty arrangement of dried flowers is a lovely idea for somebody with an autumn or winter birthday. You can pick grasses and seedheads in the country or you can dry flowers from your own garden; it's fun and quite easy. Or you can buy them, though of course it's more expensive that way! Cut the dried plants all the same length.

Bunch the flowers together; when you're happy with them, wrap sticky tape around the stalks. Hide the tape by winding ribbon over it. Tie ribbon round the parcel, finish off with a knot, and attach the little bouquet by tying its trailing ribbons over the knot; trim the ends of the bouquet ribbon away. Using the ends of the other ribbon, finish off by making a pretty bow over the bouquet.

What a lovely bonus to receive with a gift — a beautiful fresh flower. This works most effectively with a long, thin present, showing off a single bloom to perfection. First choose your flower. Trim off any excess leaves and, in the case of roses, thorns. You should end up with just one sprig of leaves.

To prevent the flower from staining the gift wrap or making it damp, wrap the end of the stalk with cling film (plastic wrap). Then cut a narrow strip of matching gift wrap; wrap it around the length of the stalk, fixing it at the back with tape. Cut a small 'V' shape at the top of the paper tube, and attach the bloom to the parcel with double-sided tape.

Craft foil is the perfect material for creating this decoration. Use a compass to draw four circles; the ones shown here measure 8cm (3in), 6.5cm (2½in) 5cm (2in) and 4cm (1½in) in diameter. Draw an inner ring of 2cm (¾in) in the centre of each circle. Rule lines to divide the circles evenly into eighths; cut along the lines to the inner circle to make eight segments.

Roll each segment of the circle into a cone; use a dab of glue to secure it. Make sure that each cone shape has a good sharp point by rolling it fairly tightly. The process is a bit fiddly; you may find it easier to roll each cone around the point of a stencil to give it shape. Repeat with the other circles.

Starting with the largest star shape, glue all the stars inside each other, positioning the points of each star between those of the preceding ones. When the glue is dry, gently bend each cone of the middle two stars towards the centre, to fill in the central space, so forming a semi-circular three-dimensional star.

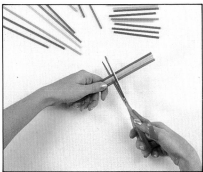

Brightly-coloured drinking straws lend themselves to decorating presents. Look for colours to co-ordinate with your gift wrap. The straws can be made of paper or plastic; both work well. Select the colours you want and cut four straws in half; discard one of each half. Cut another four straws in two, leaving one section slightly longer than the other; retain both pieces.

Place four halves, one of each colour, together over a central point in a star shape and staple them together. Do the same with the other slightly longer straws and their shorter counterparts so that you end up with three stars of slightly different sizes. With the smallest on top and largest on the bottom, staple all three together. Attach the triple star to the parcel with double-sided tape.

A TISSUE POSY

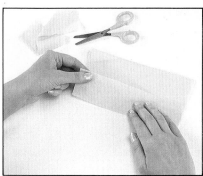

These flowers will pretty up any parcel at very little cost — they're made from tissue hankies. Open out a tissue, and fold it in half lengthwise. Trim away half of the top layer (that is, a quarter of the tissue) along the whole length as shown — this prevents the 'stalk' of the finished flower from being too bulky.

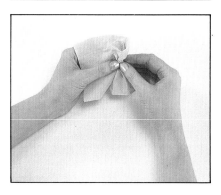

Tuck in the top corner of one end very slightly and gather up the tissue in very small pleats, gradually turning the 'flower' round as you go. When the gathering is completed, fold in the top corner of the end of the tissue as before.

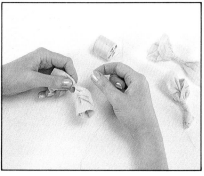

Give the 'stalk' a couple of twists to make it firm. Bind it tightly with thread and tie it securely. Make as many flowers as you need for your gift — you can make an entire bouquet if you like and wrap it up in a paper doily. Tie the flowers together with a ribbon, make a bow and attach the bouquet to your present.

P aper fans are simple to make but can look stunning, used either singly or in a row to create a ruffle around your gift. Cut a strip of paper the width you'd like the fan to be when opened, and three times the length. Fold it in half widthways, then fold it up in small even pleats, starting with the folded end. Get a sharp crease along the pleats by running them firmly between your fingers.

When you have pleated the entire length, hold the pleats together with the folded edge of the strip on top. Bend the fan in half and stick the two folded edges together with sticky tape along their length as shown. Make sure that the tape continues right to the outer edge so that the join cannot be seen when the fan is open.

Open out the fan and apply double-sided tape to its flat side; stick the fan in position on your gift. Care is needed in deciding how big to make the fan — too big and the present will be swamped, too small and it will look insignificant. It might be worthwhile experimenting with rough fans cut from newspaper first, to get the scale right before cutting your gift wrap.

An added bonus on this gift is the sweet-smelling pouch of pot-pourri. Select some fabric which will tone with your gift wrapping paper. The fabric should be fine, but not loosely woven; the scent of the pot-pourri can then easily diffuse through the material, but the petals and dust can't. Cut out a piece of fabric measuring about 15-20cm (6-8in) square.

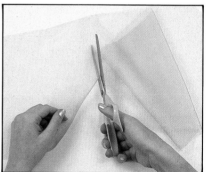

Put enough pot-pourri in the centre of the fabric to make a generous sachet — a good handful should be just right. If you can, choose a perfume which will match your present — rose pot-pourri would be ideal for a rose bowl, lavender for lavender-scented soaps. You could even use dried herbs to create a bouquet garni for a cookery book!

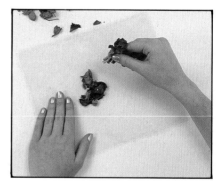

Pick up the four corners of the fabric to form a bundle. Wind sewing thread tightly around the neck of the bundle, and knot the thread securely. Tie the pot-pourri bunch very firmly in case the recipient uses the bag later in her wardrobe. Hide the thread by tying a piece of ribbon around it to match the ribbon on the parcel. Tie the pot-pourri to the gift using a little more matching ribbon.

A sweet treat for children of all ages! Boiled sweets (hard candies) with plain cellophane wrappers look best because of their clear colours, but you can use alternatives such as toffees or peppermints. Select five or six of the chosen sweets, and hold them in a bunch by one end of their wrappers.

Take a narrow piece of ribbon and tie all the sweets together tightly; if the wrappers are a little short it may help to bind them first with sewing thread. Leave a reasonably long piece of ribbon on each side of the bunch of sweets so that you can attach it easily to the parcel.

Tie the same ribbon around the parcel, leaving the ends long, then tie the sweets to the centre point as shown. Curl up each ribbon end by pulling it gently along the open blade of a pair of scissors. Try to co-ordinate your gift wrap with the chosen confectionery — black and white paper with humbugs, for example, would look very attractive.

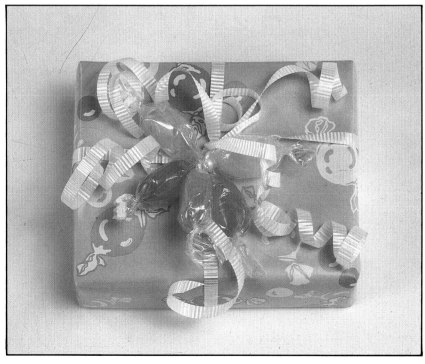

It's important that your gift is labelled clearly so that the right present goes to the right person — and that that person knows who the present is from! But there's no need to deface the wrapping paper on your gift by scrawling your message all over it.

Any well-wrapped gift needs a proper tag. It's easy to make one to go with your gift wrap; five methods are suggested in this section. Or perhaps you could tailor-make a tag especially designed for the person receiving the gift. And what a novelty to be able to *eat* the tag afterwards — well, here you will find two kinds of edible tags.

Personal and original gift tags really do
make a difference to the finished parcel,
as this selection demonstrates. And with a
little flair and imagination you can create
a wide range of attractive designs.

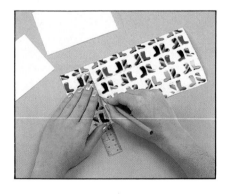

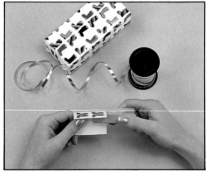

Give your presents a co-ordinated appearance by creating matching tags. For simple fold-over tags you need to select wrapping paper which has a small design. Take a piece of gift wrap and rule a rectangle on it, twice the width of the required tag. (Outline a section of the design where the motif is visible when isolated.) Ensure the corners are perfect right angles, then cut the tag out.

Paste the tag on to thin cardboard; choose a colour which picks up a shade in the gift wrap. When the glue is dry, cut around the piece of gift wrap. Fold the card in half and punch a hole in the corner. Thread a ribbon through the hole and tie it on to the gift. Alternatively, you can cut out a single image, stick it on to cardboard and cut around the outline, as with the panda tag.

If you have a long message for the recipient of your gift, this fold-out tag allows lots of room. Select a gift wrap design that has a fairly large repeat. One motif must have sufficient space around it so that it can be cut out without including any others. Draw a rectangle around the motif, ensuring that all the corners are right angles.

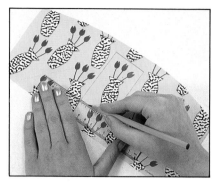

Cut the rectangle out with a craft knife. Next, cut out a piece of thin cardboard the same height as the chosen motif and exactly three times its width. Fold the cardboard in three widthways, creasing the folds well, then fold the top two sections back on themselves, as shown. Mark the folds in pencil first to be sure they are straight.

Cut the motif from the gift wrap precisely in half. Glue each half on to the top two sections of the folded card. They should fit exactly, but if necessary trim the top and bottom to form a straight edge. Try matching the colours of the lining cardboard with the gift wrap; in the example shown here, red or even black cardboard could have been used, instead of white, for a different effect.

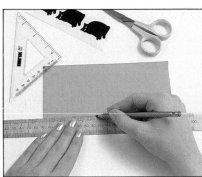

There is such a variety of stickers on the market that you're sure to find one which will make an ideal label for your gift. Take a piece of thin coloured cardboard; this will form the background for the sticker. Draw a rectangle on to the cardboard, twice the width you wish the finished tag to be.

Cut out the rectangle with a craft knife and score down the centre to form the fold; crease well. Remove the sticker from its backing and place it in position on the front of the tag. Punch a hole in the back 'page' of the tag, near the fold. Write your message inside and hang the tag on the gift.

Used greeting cards can often be turned into very acceptable gift tags. Sometimes, as here, the design lends itself to forming a tag. Cut very carefully around the lines of the motif you want to use. Make a hole with a punch, thread a ribbon through the hole and no one would guess the tag had a previous life!

Sometimes a little imagination is needed to give the tag a new and ready-made look. Here, the shape of the tag is outlined on the cardboard in red with a felt-tipped pen. Draw the outline lightly in pencil first to be absolutely sure it is the right size and shape to create the finished label.

There can be no doubt who these presents are for! It's fun to make a tag out of the initial or — even better — the whole name of the recipient. First draw the shape of the letters you want on to a piece of tracing paper. Make sure that the letters in a name interlock sufficiently.

When you're happy with the result, trace the letters (or single initial) on to coloured cardboard, pressing hard to make a clear outline. Use a ruler where there are straight sections to a letter.

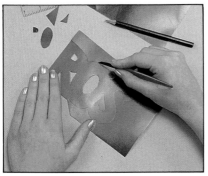

Next, cut out the shape using a craft knife, carefully following the traced lines. Punch a hole in a position where the weight of the tag will make it hang well on the gift.

A different way of matching the label to the paper is to create a larger version of a shape which appears in the gift wrap. Begin by drawing a scaled-up shape of the motif from the paper and use it as a template from which to trace the design on to the coloured cardboard.

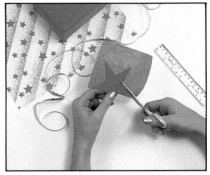

For this idea to be really effective, the colour of the tag should be as close as possible to that in the gift wrap. A layer of tissue laid over the cardboard of a near-match, as shown, might make all the difference to duplicating the final colour. Cut out the shape, and punch a hole to enable you to tie it to the gift.

Incorporate a motif from the design of your gift wrap to make a fun three-page tag. It will work with any design involving a trailing string — balloons, kites, balls of yarn and so on. The motif is stuck on the sloping top edge of the middle 'page' of the card. Cut out the motif from gift wrap. Then experiment with a sheet of white paper to get the best shape for your card.

The slanting angle of the top edge is achieved by cutting a truncated triangular shape. Having worked out the shape you want, trace around your experimental tag on to thin coloured cardboard. Don't forget to leave a bit of card protruding from the top slanting edge in the shape of the motif, as shown. Cut out the tag.

Score the two fold lines of the tag using the back of a craft knife and crease them firmly. Glue the motif in position on the middle page and draw a long string trailing down. Close the card and draw another string on the front, making sure it is continuous with the string on page two. Write the recipient's name as if it were part of that string.

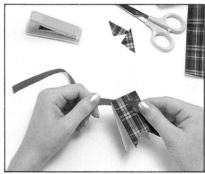

Create a stylish effect by matching the tag to the ribbon. Plain ribbon with a strongly patterned paper is attractive but a tartan ribbon with plain paper can look stunning. And if you don't have any ribbon, even a strip of fabric cut out with pinking shears will suffice! Glue a length of ribbon or fabric on to thin cardboard to make it rigid.

Trim away any excess cardboard. Fold the stiffened ribbon over and cut it to the length you want the finished tag to be. Punch a hole through your newly-created tag and thread a piece of contrasting narrow ribbon through the hole to tie it to the parcel. Trim the edges of the tag to match the ends of the bow.

One way to eat your words — or at least your name! Shortbread is the basis for these edible labels. Sift together 100g (4oz, ½ cup) of caster (fine granulated) sugar and 150g (6oz, 1½ cups) of plain flour into a bowl. Rub in 100g (4oz, ½ cup) of butter till the mixture resembles fine breadcrumbs. Add water to make a stiff dough, knead well and roll it out on a floured board.

Cut out various shapes for the tags, using either pastry cutters or paper templates. Don't forget to make the holes for threading the ribbon later. Bake at 200°C, 400°F or gas mark 6 for 15-20 minutes or until golden brown; leave to cool. Then write the name on, using icing in a piping bag, or simply with a paintbrush dipped in food colouring. This recipe will make 15-20 labels.

Children will enjoy eating these gift tags made of royal icing. Separate an egg and sift 225g (approximately ½lb, 1¼ cups) of icing (confectioner's) sugar into a bowl. Gradually add a little egg white to make a stiff dough. Knead well, then divide the mixture in two and add food colouring to one half. Knead the icing thoroughly to distribute the colouring.

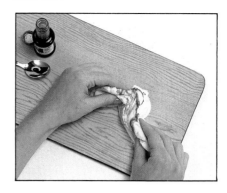

Roll out the icing to about 5mm (¼in). Cut out shapes using small pastry cutters. Colour the other portion of icing if required and repeat. Make a hole in the shapes for a ribbon, then prick out the name with a toothpick or, when the tags have dried, write the name on with a paintbrush dipped in food colouring. Leave the tags to dry out for a week. This makes about 20 tags.

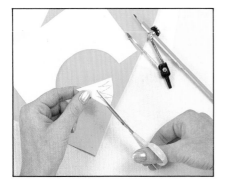

Sometimes the name tag can form the entire decoration for the gift! Wrap your gift in green paper to make a leafy-coloured background for this floral tag. Using a compass, draw a circle that will fit comfortably on top of your present. Fold it in eight and draw four daisy-shaped petals on a segment. With the circle still folded, cut the petals out. This is your template.

Draw two circles of the same diameter as the template, and trace the daisy pattern on to them; cut them out. Repeat the process with a smaller circle, to provide two inner layers for the daisy. Pile the daisies on top of each other, arranging them so that none of the petals overlaps, then stick them together in the centre with glue or double-sided tape.

Cut out a circle from yellow paper, write the recipient's name on it and fix it in the centre of the flower. Gently bend up the petals around the yellow centre. You could adapt the idea in mauves to make a Michaelmas daisy, or autumn colours for a chrysanthemum.

Victorian ladies created beautiful pictures using pressed flowers. Why not make a miniature version for a pretty gift tag? Pick up a selection of flowers and leaves and lay them face down on blotting paper. Press another layer of blotting paper on top, keeping the flowers as flat as possible. Place the flowers between the pages of a heavy book and leave them for at least a week.

Take out the flowers. Make a template for a perfect oval by folding a small sheet of paper in half and half again; draw a curve across the corner as shown and cut it out. Trace round the unfolded shape on white cardboard, and make a slightly larger oval from coloured cardboard to match the gift wrap.

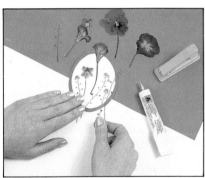

Stick the two ovals together, so that the larger one forms a frame for the tag. Arrange the pressed flowers on the white oval to your satisfaction. Glue the flowers in position, using a tube with a very fine nozzle; leave the arrangement to dry thoroughly. Punch a hole in the top of the tag, write the message on the back and tie it to the gift.

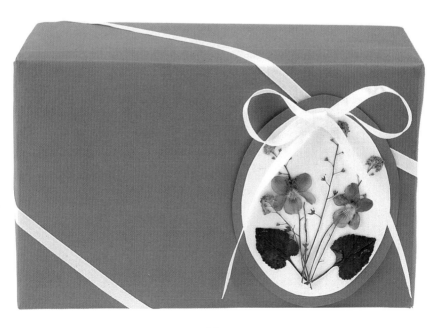

Knowing who this parcel is for is plain sailing! Fold a strip of thin cardboard in half and draw a stylized boat on to it. Cut it out and stick the ends together with tape, making a three-dimensional boat. Make two creases in the 'bottom' of the boat, along its length, to give it stability.

Cut out a paper sail. For the mast, join two cocktail sticks or toothpicks with 'tape; break off half of one of them. Stick the mast on to the sail with more tape, leaving the pointed end of the mast at the bottom.

Add a flying pennant to the top of the mast with paper, and write the recipient's name on the sail. Attach the mast by putting some Plasticine or modelling clay in the bottom of the boat; dig the mast into it. Hide the Plasticine with a small piece of cardboard to match the boat. The finishing touch is the wave made of cotton wool (known as absorbent cotton in the United States).

Any small boy who likes planes will like this label on his gift. Make some cloud-patterned gift wrap on blue paper; see page 16 for the method of spongeing. Draw the outline of a plane's body on to lightweight coloured cardboard and, on a separate sheet, the shape of its wings. Cut out both pieces.

On self-adhesive coloured paper rule two parallel lines, a little narrower than the width of the wing, and write out the name of the recipient in capital letters. The ruled lines will enable you to keep the letters to an even size.

Cut out the letters and stick them in position along the top of the wings; write who the parcel is from underneath. Cut a slot on the body of the plane to take the wings, and punch a hole in the nose. Thread a loop of ribbon through the hole and stick it to one corner of the parcel.

Usually, it's easy to guess the contents of a gift if it's a recognizable shape. But not if you disguise them! In this section, a bottle turns into a pencil, a record becomes a cushion; a cube has added interest as a dice and a circular gift becomes a hat.

Also in this section are gifts for specific occasions. The ideas in the rest of the book can, of course, be used for any present, at any time. But wrapping gifts for Christmas, weddings, christenings, Easter or Valentine's Day sometimes needs special inspiration. The following pages are bursting with stimulating and exciting ideas for all occasions.

Whether your present is for Christmas,
Valentine's Day or a christening, you can
have great fun wrapping it to match the
occasion. Or how about disguising it as a
birthday cake or a domino? No one will
ever guess what's inside.

Holly leaves are an attractive shape and perfect for decorating a festive gift. Measure the length of the diagonal across the top of your parcel. On a sheet of plain paper, draw a large holly leaf, the 'vein' of which measures slightly more than half the length of the diagonal.

Trace four holly leaves on to some green cardboard, using the template you have just created. Cut the leaves out and bend them in the middle; creasing them slightly where the central vein would be.

Make the berries from a ball of cotton wool (known as absorbent cotton in the United States) wrapped in two squares of red tissue paper. Put a dab of glue inside and twist up the tissue tightly at the base. When the glue is dry, cut off as much excess of the twist as possible. Group the leaves and berries on the parcel; attach with glue or double-sided tape.

T hese Christmas bells ring out gaily from your present. Make two paper templates, both bell-shaped, with one showing the outline of the clapper from the bottom edge. From thin cardboard, cut out two of each shape.

Cover all the cardboard shapes with gold paper (or any colour which would co-ordinate with your wrapping paper). Cover both sides, and trim away all the excess paper. On the bell shapes with the clapper, cut a slit from the curved top of the bell to the centre of the bell. On the others (the plain ones) cut a slit from the middle of the bottom edge, also to the centre.

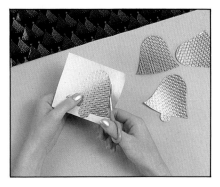

Pierce a hole in the top of the plain bell shapes and thread them with a length of ribbon. Then slot the pairs of bell shapes together (i.e. the plain one, and the one with the clapper) so that they form three-dimensional shapes, as shown here. Tie a group of as many bells as you like on to your gift. This idea can also be used for decorating a wedding gift.

Bottles of seasonal spirits make an ideal present — but hide such an obvious-looking gift under the decorative guise of a Christmas tree. Find a flower-pot just big enough to take the base of the bottle. From thin cardboard cut out a third section of a large circle and make a deep cone about 8cm (3in) shorter than the bottle. Cover the cone with suitable wrapping paper.

Put the bottle in the flower-pot and place the cone on top. You may need to trim the cone if it seems to cover too much of the flower-pot; do this with care, since you could easily make the cone too short! Double over a piece of tinsel, tie it in a knot and stick it on top of the 'tree'.

What fun for a child to see Frosty and know that the snowman's hiding a gift! Wrap up a cylindrical gift in paper to form the body of the snowman. Crush newspaper into a shape for the head and stick it on top of the gift. Cover the body with cotton wool (absorbent cotton), sticking it on with dabs of glue. Create a face from bits of paper and stick in place.

For the hat, you need a strip of cardboard, plus a circle big enough to make the brim. Draw an inner circle in the brim, the diameter of Frosty's head; cut it out to form the 'lid' of the hat. Roll the strip of cardboard up to form the crown of the hat; stick it in place with tape.

Stick on the top of the hat, then attach the brim, putting strips of tape inside the crown. Paint the hat with black poster paint; it'll need two or three coats. Wrap around the red ribbon to form a cheery hat-band and put it on Frosty's head. Fray the ends of some patterned ribbon to form a scarf and tie it firmly in place.

A three-dimensional Santa Claus tag, complete with fluffy beard, provides a jolly festive decoration on a gift. Draw a fairly large rectangle on thin red cardboard; make sure that all the corners are right angles. Score down the middle and fold the cardboard, creasing it well. Draw an inverted 'V' for Santa's hat, and a curve for his chin; cut them out with a craft knife.

Curve the hat and chin outward to give them a three-dimensional look, then draw in the eyes and mouth. Form a beard from a small piece of cotton wool (absorbent cotton), and stick it in position with a dab of glue. Do the same with the fur trim on the edge of the hat and the pom-pom on its tip. Punch a hole in the back of the label, write your message and tie the tag on the parcel.

W hy not decorate your
Christmas present as if it
were a Christmas tree — with
glittering baubles and tinsel? Wrap
the gift in some elegant paper;
something plain but shiny will set off
the baubles better than a more
complex Christmas design — you
could use aluminium foil. Then
thread Christmas baubles on to a
length of tinsel.

Decide where you want to put the
decoration and cover the area with a
few strips of double-sided tape. If the
parcel is rectangular, put the baubles
in one corner; if the parcel is square,
the middle would be better. An
upright parcel like that shown here
looks best with the decoration on the
top. Group the baubles into a bunch
on the gift, wrapping the tinsel
around them to form a nest.

A heavenly messenger bears the greetings on this Christmas present. Cut a quarter section of a circle from light cardboard to form a narrow cone for the body. On a folded piece of paper draw one arm and one wing against the edge of the fold as shown, so that when they are cut out you will have a pair of each.

Make the cone and cover it with silver paper (aluminium foil would do). Trace the arm and wings on to silver paper; cut them out and glue them in their relevant positions on the body.

Make the head by rolling up some white tissue paper into a firm ball, twisting the ends of the tissue tightly to form a 'neck'. Glue the head into the top of the cone. Tie a scrap of tinsel into a loose knot and stick it on the head as a halo. Make a scroll from white paper, write on your message and stick it between the angel's hands. Attach the angel to the gift with double-side tape.

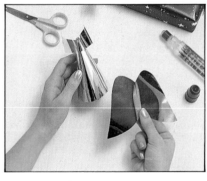

With so many presents being exchanged at this time of the year, tags become even more important. What about some special seasonal ones? Draw any festive shape you like on to thin cardboard; this one is a Christmas stocking. Cut out the shape and cover it with bright paper; try to co-ordinate the colours with those in the gift wrap you use for your present.

If your wrapping paper has a particular theme in its design make a tag to echo it. To ensure that your design is symmetrical, fold a piece of paper in half and draw on half the design against the fold. Cut around the outline through both layers of paper; open out and use this as a template for the design. Cover a piece of light cardboard with gift wrap and trace around the template.

Cut around the outline and punch a hole at the top of the tag. Write your message and tie the tag on to the parcel. You could cheat a little when designing the shape of your tag by tracing an illustration from a magazine or by using the outline of a pastry cutter.

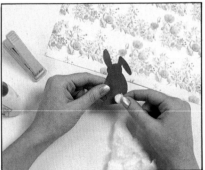

This cute rabbit tag tells the kids who their Easter present is from. Draw the shape of a rabbit on to white cardboard; if you're not good at drawing, you could cheat by tracing the outline of a rabbit from a magazine or book illustration. When you're happy with your design, cut it out.

Either paint the bunny shape, or cover it with brown paper (or whatever colour suits your gift wrap; a red or even green rabbit would be fun). Next take a piece of cotton wool (absorbent cotton) and roll it into a ball for the tail; stick it in position with a dab of glue. Make a hole in the rabbit's head for some ribbon, write your message and tie the tag to the gift.

SPRING CHICK

This cheery chick will brighten up any Easter gift. Cut two cardboard circles the same size, then cut a small circle from the centre of each to create two wide rings. Put both rings together and wind yellow yarn around them, passing the yarn through the centre. Continue doing this until the rings are well covered and the inner circle is almost full of yarn.

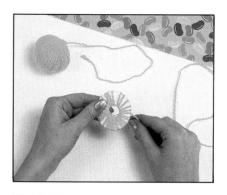

Snip through all the yarn along the outer edge of the cardboard rings. Pass a length of yarn between the two rings, wind it tightly around all the strands of yarn and tie it firmly, leaving long ends. Cut off the cardboard circles and fluff out the ball. Make a bigger ball for the body from two larger rings, and before cutting, pass a pipe cleaner through the rings to form the legs.

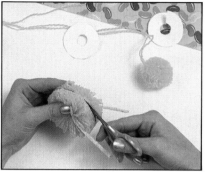

Tie the two balls together firmly. Bend the 'legs' up at the ends and wind a section of pipe cleaner around each foot leaving a V-shape on either side so that each foot now has three 'claws'; paint the feet and legs red. Make eyes and a beak out of felt and glue into position. This would work just as well with a Christmas robin decoration, using red and brown yarn.

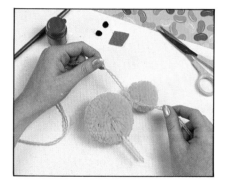

A cake, plus candle, is just the right disguise for a birthday present! First, make a drum-shaped frame for the cake; cut a strip of thin cardboard just wider than your present, curl it in a circle big enough to cover your gift and stick it in place with sticky tape. Cut a circle to fit as a lid; attach it with strips of tape.

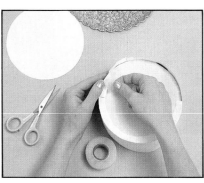

Cut a strip of white paper to cover the sides of the drum and glue it in position. Tuck one edge of the paper under the open end of the drum and trim the other edge close to the top of the drum to leave a small turning. Cut a series of small nicks in the turning and fold the flaps over, taping them to the lid. Cut a circle slightly smaller than the circumference of the drum and glue it in place.

Place the present inside the cake and put it on a cake stand. Cut two lengths of cord to fit round the circumference of the cake and glue the ends to prevent them from unravelling. Glue one piece to the top of the cake to form 'icing', and the second piece around the bottom, to fix the cake to the stand. Finally, put the candle in the holder and pierce through the centre of the cake.

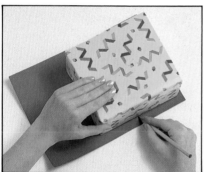

Paste the recipient's age in a great big number on the side of their present so that *everybody* knows how old they are! Draw around the present, so that you know exactly what size the numbers must be to fill the side of the gift and make a big impact.

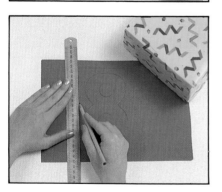

Draw the appropriate number using a ruler and measure carefully. Choose thin cardboard or plain paper in a contrasting colour to the wrapping paper.

Cut the numbers out and stick them in position on your gift. You could make a numerical tag to match. This idea could be adapted for use with gifts celebrating wedding anniversaries — 25, 50 and so on.

This heart of woven paper can hold a Valentine's Day gift. Lightweight paper in contrasting colours gives the best effect. Cut a strip of paper 25cm by 10cm (10in by 4in) and draw the template on page 127 on to it. Cut the shape out and fold it in half. Then cut the two slits as indicated on the template. Repeat with another strip of paper in a different colour.

Hold a section of the heart in each hand, as shown, with the strips pointing upwards. Weave the two sections together, starting with the two inner strips. You need to open out each strip to slot the other strip through it, as illustrated.

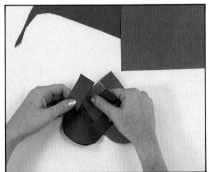

Continue doing this until all the strips are interwoven. It is fairly fiddly but does work; it's clear at this stage why you need lightweight but strong paper! The finished item will open out like a basket, so that it can hold small gifts. The basket would also be very pretty made in felt.

Aromantic padded heart containing a little gift is perfect to give on Valentine's Day! Cut out two heart shapes from cardboard, one about 4cm (1½in) larger all round than the other. From red lining fabric, cut out a heart shape a little bigger than the larger heart. Take a gift box, wrap it in cotton wool (absorbent cotton) and place it on top of the smaller heart.

When there's enough padding, cover the heart in the red lining, stretching it over the heart shape and sticking it firmly in position on the back with plenty of tape. You'll need to snip the fabric around the inverted point of the heart so that the fabric can open out to fit properly.

Cover the larger heart in white tissue paper, otherwise the brown surface may show through the lacey doily. Cut off a frill of about 5cm (2in) from the edge of four or five doilies, and pleat them up around the edge of the large heart, fixing them with tape as shown. When the whole heart has been edged like this, apply some strong glue to the middle and place the padded heart in position.

This simple but effective idea is just right for a wedding. Cover your gift with plain paper. Buy some rose petal-shaped confetti. Alternatively, you could make the petals yourself from softly-coloured tissue paper: fold a piece of tissue into about eight and cut out an oval shape; repeat for as many petals as you need.

Arrange a cluster in a flower-shape on each corner of the gift. Stick each petal into position with a small dab of glue right at one end of the petal. When the glue is dry, bend up the petals to give a 3-dimensional effect. You could use this idea for a silver anniversary gift by wrapping the parcel in aluminium foil and using petals of just one colour.

A gift wrapped up as a prayer book makes an unusual and moving present for a wedding or confirmation. Wrap up the gift in gold paper so that it will look like the closed pages of the book. The last flap should not be folded in the usual way, but should be cut precisely to fit the side of the gift as shown; glue it in place.

Take two pieces of thick cardboard slightly larger than the size of the gift. You will also need a long strip of thin cardboard measuring the width and length of the gift. Use tape to stick the thick cardboard on to either side of the thin cardboard to make a book cover for the gift. Cover the outside with plain paper as shown; glue all the edges down firmly.

Spread glue over the inside of the book cover, and place the gift firmly on one side of it. Wrap the cover over the other side of the gift, making sure it's stuck properly. Cut out gold crosses (or other appropriate symbols relevant for your recipient's religion) and stick them in place. This idea is also good for a christening or anniversary gift.

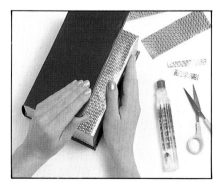

This pretty cradle makes a charming decoration for a baby girl's christening present. From thin cardboard, cut out a small box shape to make the framework for the crib. Fold up the sides and stick them in place with tape.

Cut a piece of ribbon one and a half times the length of the perimeter of the cot. Sew the ends together to make a loop, and run a gathering thread around the top. Apply some glue to the outside of the box and put the gathered frill over it, positioning it on the lower half. Repeat with more ribbon, sticking the frill over the first one, right at the top edge of the box.

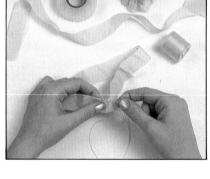

Put some cotton wool (absorbent cotton), a scrap of lace and a piece of wide ribbon in the cradle. Take another piece of ribbon, wider than that used for the frills, and cut a strip long enough to make a canopy. Cut a matching strip of cardboard; spread it with glue and cover with the ribbon. Fold it in half and stick in position over one end of the crib.

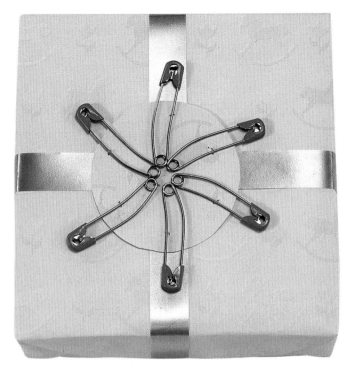

A new mother always needs lots of nappy (diaper) pins, so give her a selection on top of her new baby's gift! Use a compass or trace round a suitable circular object to draw a circle on thin cardboard, with a matching circle of gift wrap. Cut them out and glue them together.

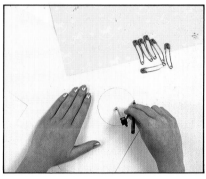

Get some safety nappy pins. Choose blue ones for a boy, pink for a girl. Decide how you'd like to arrange the series of safety pins; radiating out from the centre probably forms the most interesting pattern.

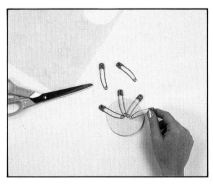

Thread a large sharp needle with sewing thread to match the gift wrap and sew the pins in place. Make sure you get the position of each stitch right first time; extra holes made by the needle will look awful! Wrap the parcel, tie some ribbon around it and stick the pin-circle on top with glue or double-sided tape.

J ust the disguise if you're giving a
cylinder-shaped gift to a child —
the famous British red pillar-box
(mailbox). You could of course adapt
the idea and make a rocket, for
example. Cut a strip of thin red
cardboard to fit around your gift;
secure it around the gift with sticky
tape. Draw a circle for the lid, larger
than the diameter of the cylinder; cut
a line to its centre as shown.

Overlap the cut edges slightly to
form a shallow cone, then fix with
sticky tape on the wrong side. Wrap
one end of the post-box with black
paper, folding it over to prevent the
present from falling out. Put double-
sided tape around the inside of the
lid and stick in position. Add a
narrow black rectangle for the
posting slit and a white rectangle for
the notice of collection times.

Any little girl would be thrilled if her present looked like a hat. This idea obviously will only work on a gift that is circular and flat, so that the gift itself can form the crown. Cut a brim from a circle of thin cardboard and cover it with a circle of plain, pastel-coloured paper. Wrap the present by rolling it in matching paper, as shown.

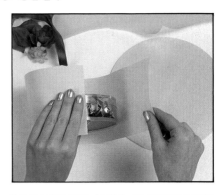

Make sure the paper fits tightly around the base by folding it in a series of small triangles. Trim the turning on the top of the gift to leave a small edge; fold that in neat triangles too. Stick the triangles down on to each other with tape, making sure that the surface is left as flat as possible.

Place the gift in the centre of the brim and stick it in position with glue or double-sided tape. Cut another circle of wrapping paper slightly smaller than the diameter of the crown; glue it in place. Tie a ribbon around the junction of the crown and brim, leaving the ends trailing. Cut a 'V' in the ribbon ends and glue on a couple of artificial flowers for a finishing touch.

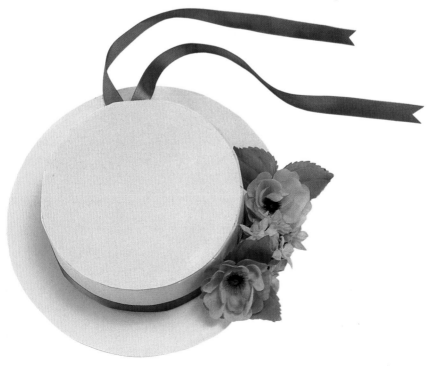

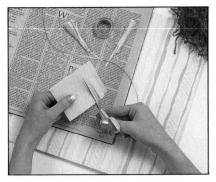

Disguise the unmistakable shape of a record by making it look like a cushion. First create paper tassels. Cut a piece of coloured paper into narrow strips leaving about 2.5cm (1in) at the bottom uncut so that you create a fringe. Roll up the fringe, catching in a short length of narrow ribbon. Secure the tassel with coloured tape.

Take some wrapping paper that is more than twice the size of the gift, fold it in half around the record and cut it so that it is just a little larger. Join two of the sides together with coloured tape along their full length, attaching the ends of the tassels at the corners as you do so. Put a strip of tape over the folded edge of the 'bag'.

Stuff the inside of the 'bag' on both sides of the record with shredded tissue, being careful to put some in the corners. Don't use too much or the wrapping paper will wrinkle. Seal along the remaining open edge with tape.

Here's another clever idea for disguising a record. Get two large squares of cardboard; the side of a box will do. Position the record in one corner as shown and draw a line from the bottom right corner of the record to the top right corner of the cardboard. Draw a second rule from the top left corner of the record to complete the kite shape. Repeat for the other square.

Cut out the shapes and sandwich the record between them. Cover one side in coloured paper, folding over the edges and fixing them with sticky tape on the reverse. Cut another piece of paper slightly smaller than the cardboard shape; glue it in position on the back of the kite.

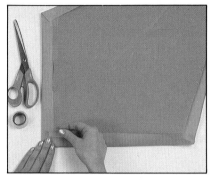

Draw two lines joining the four corners of the kite, and put contrasting tape along them; take care not to stretch the tape as it will pucker the paper. Cut out as many paper bow shapes as you want for the kite's tail. Attach the bows with double-sided tape or glue to a length of ribbon and stick the tail in position behind the longest point of the kite.

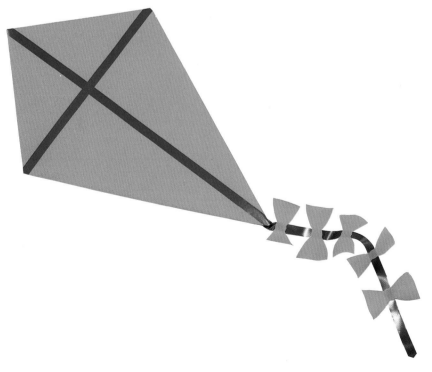

Make a small present look that extra bit special — and that extra bit bigger! Wrap the gift into a ball shape, then cut a strip of paper about three times the width of the gift and long enough to form loops on each side of it. Fold the edges over. Gather small pleats at each end, securing them with sticky tape. Pinch-pleat four gathers in the middle of the strip and secure.

For the trailing sections of the bow, cut a five-sided piece of paper as shown. Fold over the edges in to the centre at the back and secure with tape. Gather pinch pleats at one end and secure. At the other end cut out a V-shaped section to form a nicely-shaped tail. Repeat the procedure a second time.

Turn the pleated ends of the long strip to the middle to form the loops, and secure with double-sided tape. Stick the tails under the bow with more tape. Finally, put double-sided tape over the join on top of the bow and stick the gift in position. Puff out the loops so they look nice and full.

Disguise a bottle as a pencil and keep the recipient guessing! Make a cylinder, about 5cm (2in) shorter than the bottle, from light cardboard, join the sides with tape. Draw a third section of a circle—about 7.5cm (3in) radius—on pale cardboard and cut it out. Roll it in to a cone shape, running the flat edge of a pair of scissors along it to help it curl. Tape in place.

Make a small cone for the lead of the pencil and glue it on to the larger cone. Attach several lengths of sticky tape to the inside edge of the cone and, putting your arm inside the cylinder, stick the tape down to hold the cone in position. Fit the pencil over the bottle and secure with two strips of tape across the bottom.

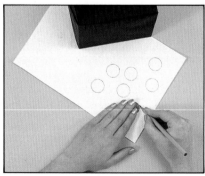

Cube-shaped presents will look more interesting disguised as dice — and it's fun if a small, flat gift becomes a domino. For the dice, make sure the gift is a perfect cube by measuring it; the idea won't work well unless it is. Cover the gift with black paper. Then draw several circles on white paper; an easy way of doing this is by tracing the outline of a suitably sized coin.

Cut out the circles carefully and lay them on the box; glue them in place. Look at a real dice to get the juxtaposition of the sides correct. The domino can be treated in the same way.

Brighten up a dull-looking, flat gift by turning it into a playing card. Wrap the present in plain white paper. Make a template for the spade by folding a piece of paper in half and drawing half the outline against the fold; this way the design will be symmetrical. Trace around the template on to black paper and cut the shape out. Stick the spade in the centre of the 'card'.

Cut two small spades for the corner designs. Then, using a ruler, draw an 'A' in two of the corners, being careful to make them both the same. Glue the small spades underneath. Cut a piece of patterned paper — smaller than the card — and stick it on the back. You could vary the idea by making the King or Queen of Hearts for your husband or wife, or the ten of clubs for a ten-year-old.

BOX TEMPLATES

The following are designs for the various boxes described in the 'Boxes and Bags' section of this book, plus one heart-shaped design from 'Special Occasions'. Draw the templates out carefully, following either the metric or the imperial measurements — do not use a combination of both. To score the fold lines run along the dotted lines — on the inside of the box — with the back of a craft knife or the blunt edge of a pair of scissors; this will help you to fold the box more easily. If you wish to increase or decrease the size of your box just scale the measurements up or down as required.

Squared Up (page 32)

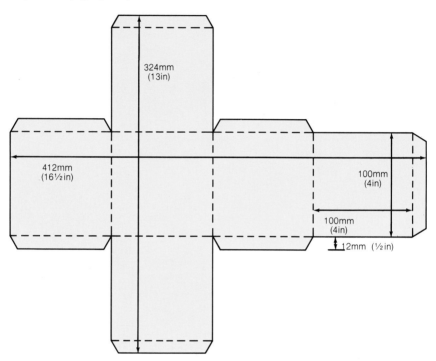

Box Clever (page 33)

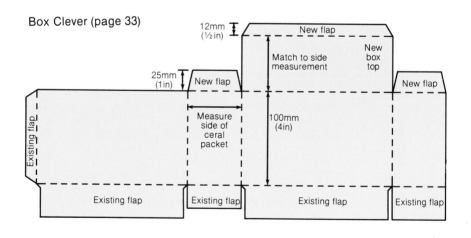

Diamonds Are Forever (page 34)

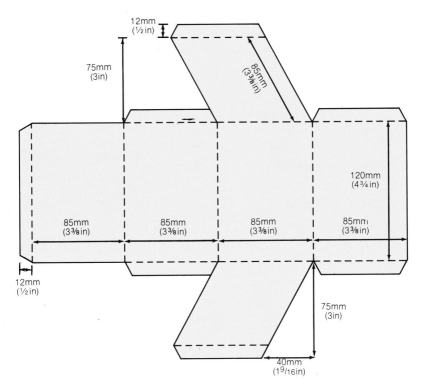

Floral Tribute (page 36)

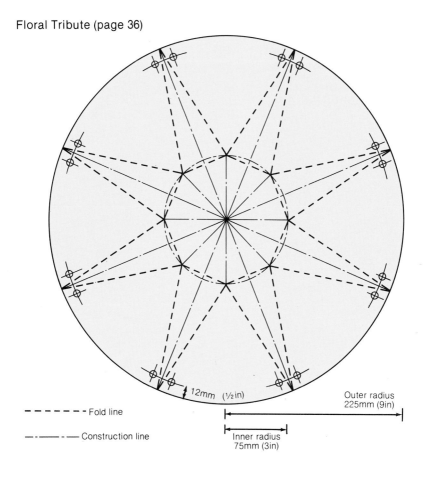

- - - - - - Fold line

—·—·—·— Construction line

12mm (½in)

Outer radius
225mm (9in)

Inner radius
75mm (3in)

Handle With Care! (page 37)

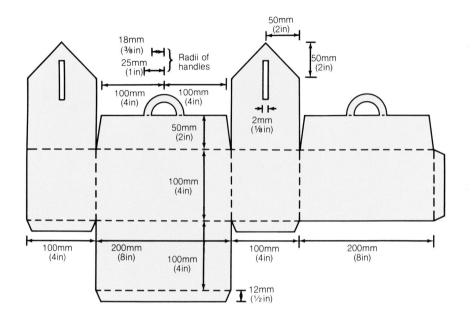

The Pyramids (page 39)

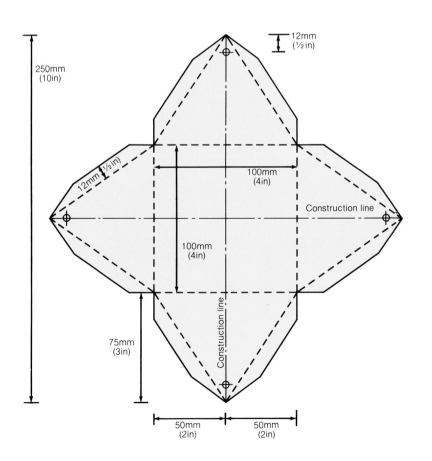

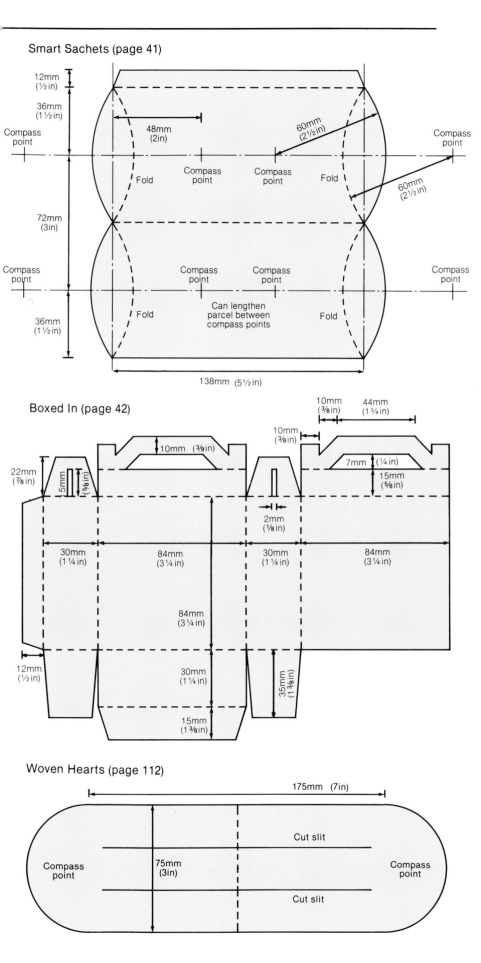

Smart Sachets (page 41)

12mm (½ in)
36mm (1½ in)
Compass point
48mm (2in)
60mm (2½ in)
Compass point
Fold
Compass point
Compass point
Fold
60mm (2½ in)
72mm (3in)
Compass point
Compass point
Compass point
Compass point
36mm (1½ in)
Fold
Can lengthen parcel between compass points
Fold
138mm (5½ in)

Boxed In (page 42)

10mm (⅜ in)   44mm (1¾ in)
10mm (⅜ in)
10mm (⅜ in)
10mm (⅜ in)
22mm (⅞ in)
5mm (³⁄₁₆ in)
7mm (¼ in)
15mm (⅝ in)
2mm (⅛ in)
30mm (1¼ in)
84mm (3¼ in)
30mm (1¼ in)
84mm (3¼ in)
84mm (3¼ in)
12mm (½ in)
30mm (1¼ in)
35mm (1⅜ in)
15mm (1⅜ in)

Woven Hearts (page 112)

175mm (7in)
Cut slit
Compass point
75mm (3in)
Compass point
Cut slit

INDEX

ACKNOWLEDGEMENTS

The publishers would like to thank the following for their
help in compiling this book:

Hallmark Cards Ltd, Hallmark House, Station Road,
Henley-on-Thames, Oxfordshire

The House of Mayfair, Cramlington, Northumberland
(Manufacturers of Fablon self-adhesive plastic)

Paperchase Ltd, 213 Tottenham Court Road, London W1